I0409778

CHAPTER 1: UNRAVELING THE MYSTERY OF REAL ESTATE INVESTMENT

Picture a world where bricks and mortar hold the key to your dreams, a tangible realm where the ordinary transforms into something extraordinary. Welcome to the captivating world of real estate investment, where possibilities abound, and the physical meets the imaginative.

Let's start with the basics - real estate comprises all the physical land and structures on our planet. Unlike digital assets like stocks and bonds, real estate exists in the real world, solid and tangible. It offers a wealth of opportunities to investors who can build, develop, or enhance properties to create value and profits.

The way a property is used, maintained, and owned significantly impacts the local economy. A well-kept neighborhood tends to increase the value of homes, while a neglected community can lead to decreased property values. Understanding this relationship between property and environment is crucial for savvy real estate investors.

Real estate comes in four main types: plots of land, residential, commercial, and industrial. Each type offers unique opportunities in the real estate market. While we'll focus mainly on residential multifamily homes, it's essential to grasp the different dimensions of real estate.

Plots of land are blank canvases of potential, regardless of whether they are vacant lots or farms waiting for development. They can become lucrative investments if you foresee future development or find the perfect location for a business venture.

Residential properties cater to people looking for a place to call home. They range from single-family houses to condos and multifamily residences. Investors can rent out homes, wholesale properties, or turn them into vacation rentals.

Commercial real estate revolves around properties used for business purposes. Hotels, apartments, hospitals, and more fall under this category. Investing in commercial properties requires careful planning due to different rules and regulations.

Industrial real estate involves warehouses, manufacturing facilities, and research spaces. These properties serve as essential support for businesses and organizations.

Entering the world of real estate investment might seem overwhelming at first, with complex legal terms and intricacies to navigate. But with dedication and understanding, anyone can find success in this field.

The real estate market is more than just buying and selling properties. It involves a network of professionals, such as property managers, appraisers, and legal advisors, who contribute to its growth and sustainability.

As you delve deeper into real estate investment, you'll discover various strategies.

Residential properties can be flipped, wholesaled, or rented out for passive income. Additionally, properties can appreciate over time, allowing investors to sell at a higher price or leverage the equity for further investments.

Modern investors can explore other avenues like Real Estate Investment Trusts (REITs) or Mortgage-Backed Securities (MBS). REITs allow investors to pool funds to invest in a diverse portfolio of properties managed by a company. On the other hand, MBS enables investors to profit from the mortgage market without the hassle of property management.

In this exciting journey, you hold the power to transform tangible dreams into reality. Real estate investment offers boundless possibilities and rewards for those willing to take the plunge. So embrace the challenge, seize the opportunities, and embark on an adventure into the captivating realm of real estate.

CHAPTER 2: EMBRACING REAL ESTATE INVESTMENT – A MULTIFAMILY ODYSSEY

Congratulations! You've taken your first steps into the captivating world of real estate investment. But hold on tight, for there's a whole universe of opportunities awaiting you. Let's embark on an exhilarating journey into the realm of multifamily properties—a realm that holds the key to unparalleled financial prosperity and a wealth of exciting possibilities.

In the world of real estate, there are no barriers to entry; anyone, regardless of their background or expertise, can succeed if they're willing to put in the effort. Whether you're seeking hands-on involvement or prefer a more passive approach, real estate offers a myriad of avenues to suit your preferences. Want to invest in physical properties without dealing with maintenance or management? Employ a professional management company or consider the world of Real Estate Investment Trusts (REITs) for a "hands-off" strategy.

Or perhaps the thrill of renovation and crafting excites you, beckoning you towards the path of house-flipping and property renovation.

Real estate investment is limited only by your imagination and work ethic. But what are the compelling reasons to dive headlong into this world of opportunities? Let's explore seven solid reasons that will leave you convinced that real estate investment is a formidable financial decision.

Reason 1: Diversify Your Portfolio In the vast ocean of finance, diversity is the guiding star. Diversifying your portfolio ensures that your assets are not all tied to one ship. While stocks and other assets can be volatile, real estate provides a rock-solid foundation of stability. Owning different types of real estate offers a hedge against potential risks. If one investment falters, others may rise to the occasion, minimizing potential losses.

Reason 2: Take Control of Your Investment Unlike many other forms of investment, real estate puts the reins firmly in your hands.

You have complete control over how your property is managed, maintained, and utilized. From choosing tenants to deciding on upgrades and renovations, every aspect of your investment is under your direct supervision. As you hold onto your property over time, the market's ebbs and flows can work in your favor, building equity and securing your financial future.

Reason 3: Harness the Power of Leverage Real estate investors wield a powerful tool called leverage. By borrowing funds to purchase properties, investors can multiply their returns without relying solely on their own capital. As property values increase, the equity builds, enabling investors to leverage these assets to acquire additional properties and expand their portfolio further. Leveraging smartly and patiently can lead to impressive returns on your investment.

Reason 4: Maximize Your Tax Benefits One of the biggest perks of real estate investment lies in the realm of tax benefits. Property owners enjoy numerous deductions and credits that can significantly reduce their taxable income.

Expenses related to property management, insurance, property taxes, and more can all be deducted, empowering you to make strategic financial moves that enhance your overall returns.

Reason 5: Strengthen Your Cash Flow Real estate investments are a wellspring of steady cash flow. Rental income generated from your properties provides a consistent stream of revenue that grows as you pay off mortgages and build equity. Additionally, with smart tax planning and expense management, you can maximize your cash flow potential.

Reason 6: Invest in Tangible Assets with Enduring Value Unlike volatile stocks or depreciating assets like cars, real estate holds enduring value. Even during market downturns, properties maintain their intrinsic worth. Owning real estate means you possess a tangible asset with the potential to appreciate over time, leading to substantial returns on your investment.

Reason 7: Experience the Power of Appreciation Appreciation, the art of a property's value rising over time, is a fundamental characteristic of real estate investment.

As properties appreciate, investors can enjoy increased rental income or capitalize on the property's higher market value by selling it for a profit. Many investors adopt the "buy and hold" strategy, allowing properties to appreciate over the long term and significantly enhance their wealth.

As we step into the timeless debate of real estate versus stocks, we recognize that both investment avenues offer unique advantages. Stocks offer liquidity and flexibility, while real estate embodies stability and longevity. The true power of real estate investment lies in multifamily properties—a domain that blends the best of both worlds.

Investing in multifamily properties unlocks unparalleled potential. The allure of multifamily properties lies in their ability to generate multiple streams of income from a single asset. Owning a multifamily property means housing multiple tenants under one roof, significantly boosting rental income and cash flow.

Beyond financial rewards, multifamily properties offer the opportunity for community-building and nurturing lasting relationships with tenants. Investing in multifamily properties is more than a mere financial decision; it's a chance to create a positive impact on the lives of those who call your property home.

The journey of multifamily investment awaits you, filled with exciting challenges and boundless rewards. As you step into this realm, remember that real estate investment is not just about bricks and mortar; it's about embracing the power of possibility and transforming it into enduring prosperity. Let's explore the multifamily properties domain together, unlocking the secrets to financial freedom and a world of boundless opportunities.

CHAPTER 3: UNLOCKING THE POWER OF MULTIFAMILY REAL ESTATE

Embarking on a journey into the world of real estate investment is an exciting endeavor, but the real challenge lies in choosing the right type of property to invest in. Among the myriad options, multifamily real estate emerges as a shining star, offering unparalleled appeal and a wealth of opportunities. In this chapter, let's explore the fascinating world of multifamily real estate, understanding its history, diverse categories, and the undeniable power it holds for investors like you.

Multifamily real estate encompasses two key categories: Commercial and Residential. Our focus will be on residential multifamily homes, which consist of dwellings with less than five units, such as duplexes or quadplexes. These properties boast a rich history, dating back to pre-World War II, when grand apartment buildings with high ceilings and lavish materials were constructed. Following the war, suburban living gained popularity, and multifamily homes offered an affordable and communal lifestyle.

Today, multifamily real estate includes both commercial properties and residential homes with multiple units, catering to diverse needs and preferences. Investors are drawn to residential multifamily homes for their significant potential for return on investment. Beyond the financial allure, these properties appeal to multigenerational families seeking cohabitation with privacy or astute investors keen on "house hacking" – living in one unit while renting out the others for additional income.

Distinguishing multifamily real estate from single-family homes is essential to grasp the unique advantages it offers. While residential multifamily homes boast multiple livable units and separate addresses, single-family homes consist of a single livable unit with a solitary address. The key distinction lies in the ability of multifamily properties to multiply income and appreciation potential through rental rates and occupancy.

The power of multifamily real estate as an attractive investment option lies in several compelling reasons:

Growing Your Real Estate Portfolio: Adding a multifamily property instantly diversifies and strengthens your real estate portfolio, accelerating your wealth-building journey.

Property Management Options: Managing a multifamily property becomes more viable due to increased rental income, allowing for smarter financial decisions.

Cash Flow: Multifamily properties are a treasure trove of cash flow potential, providing steady income even if one unit becomes vacant.

Tax Benefits: Real estate's inherent tax advantages are amplified in multifamily properties, offering substantial deductions and financial benefits.

Appreciation Potential: While appreciation applies to both single-family and multifamily properties, the latter allows for unique strategies like "live-in appreciation," leveraging the property's growth while residing in it.

However, multifamily investment is not without its challenges. Running and maintaining such properties require significant effort, and competition for affordable multifamily homes can be fierce, especially for newcomers.

Despite these hurdles, the benefits far outweigh the drawbacks for astute investors who seize the opportunity.

So, how does investing in multifamily real estate pave the way to financial freedom? The answer lies in generating passive income that exceeds your monthly expenses. Financial freedom is achieved when your passive income reaches or surpasses your monthly lifestyle costs.

Let's explore a scenario: You invest in a duplex, conservatively renting both units. By scaling this approach and adding more multifamily units to your portfolio, your passive income multiplies, inching you closer to financial freedom.

Before embarking on your multifamily investment journey, it's essential to have a clear vision and strategy in place. Conduct thorough research, educate yourself on the nuances of multifamily real estate, and devise a solid plan for your investment endeavors.

As you set forth on the path of multifamily real estate, remember that the key to success lies in making informed decisions and embracing the opportunities that lie ahead. Financial freedom awaits those bold enough to venture into this realm, where small steps can lead to extraordinary returns and a life of limitless possibilities.

CHAPTER 4: THE M.A.G.I.C. APPROACH TO MULTIFAMILY REAL ESTATE

As you delve into the realm of real estate investment, the allure of multifamily properties captures your imagination. But before embarking on this exciting journey, let's take a moment to explore the essential elements that will set you up for success in this dynamic market.

Mastering the Real Estate Landscape

Before making any significant investment, understanding the lay of the land is crucial. Multifamily homes have earned a reputation as stable and lucrative investments, especially during economic downturns. Their ability to generate consistent income, even in challenging times, makes them a favorite among investors seeking security.

In recent years, multifamily properties have experienced an unprecedented surge in demand, driving property values to new heights. Even amidst the uncertainty of the 2020 pandemic, multifamily homes stood strong, buoyed by government support and stimulus packages. Contrary to expectations, tenants continued to meet their rental obligations, contributing to the sector's unwavering performance.

Mastery of Finances and Strategic Management

While the multifamily market appears promising, comprehending the financial intricacies and implementing smart management practices is paramount. Financing a multifamily property is often more accessible than securing funding for a single-family home. Banks view these properties as lower-risk investments, given the potential for multiple income streams.

The M.A.G.I.C. approach helps you navigate the financial landscape with ease:

> Multiple Income Potential: Recognize the power of multiple income streams from a single multifamily property.
> Ample Returns: Understand how the property's cap rate impacts your returns and guides your investment decisions.
> Growth and Value: Assess the property's growth potential and long-term value to ensure a fruitful investment.
> Innovative Financing: Explore creative financing options to maximize your investment and capitalize on opportunities.

Comprehensive Management: Implement a strategic management plan to sustain and enhance the property's value.

Multifamily Real Estate Trends: A Glimpse into 2022

The world of real estate is ever-evolving, and staying ahead of trends is paramount. Analyzing multifamily real estate trends in 2022 provides valuable insights, aiding you in anticipating future developments and opportunities. Despite challenges posed by the pandemic and urban migration, multifamily properties remain an attractive investment option.

As millennials emerge as a significant buying force, the demand for rental properties is expected to soar, especially with rising homeownership costs.

The current supply-demand imbalance has given sellers the upper hand, but as the market stabilizes, prices are likely to adjust, presenting unique opportunities for investors.

The M.A.G.I.C. Approach Unleashed

Armed with the M.A.G.I.C. approach, your journey into multifamily real estate unlocks a world of possibilities and prosperity. As you navigate each step with wisdom and strategic acumen, the multifamily revolution embraces you with zeal. Your future in multifamily real estate awaits—a future brimming with possibilities and financial liberation!

CHAPTER 5: THE PATH TO PROSPERITY IN MULTIFAMILY REAL ESTATE

Welcome to the realm of multifamily real estate—a world of boundless opportunities and untold fortunes waiting to be discovered! As we venture forth into this captivating domain, let us uncover the five essential aspects that will pave the way to your success—N.A.V.I.G.

N - Navigating Property Selection

In Chapter 3, we glimpsed the diverse array of multifamily properties available for investment. Today, we set our sights on the smaller, yet no less enchanting, properties—duplexes, triplexes, and fourplexes. These gems will be the heart of our exploration.

A - Analyzing "-plex" Marvels

Before we proceed, let us understand the essence of these "-plexes." Whether duplexes, triplexes, or fourplexes, these properties encompass multiple units beneath a single roof, sharing walls and fostering a sense of community.

They offer the best of both worlds—a blend of commercial potential and residential comforts.

V - Valuable Advantages

The allure of "-plexes" lies in the magical advantages they offer. As the owner, you wield the power to establish rules and regulations for your tenants, ensuring a harmonious environment. Additionally, these properties often qualify for tax deductions, elevating their financial appeal.

Within the vicinity of "-plexes," tenants discover a treasure trove of amenities—lush yards, convenient access to local attractions, and reduced commute times, making them an enchanting choice for those seeking a perfect abode.

I - Investigating Potential Pitfalls

As we delve deeper into the realm of "-plexes," it is essential to acknowledge the potential challenges. Privacy may be a concern for some tenants who seek solitude in larger spaces. Furthermore, managing multiple units demands careful attention and organization.

Acquiring a "-plex" property may require substantial initial investment compared to single-family homes. Hence, it is wise to embark on this journey with eyes wide open, assessing risks and rewards alike.

G - Guiding Your Criteria

Embarking on the quest for the perfect "-plex" property requires a firm grasp of the criteria guiding your choices. Treat this endeavor as a business venture, regardless of whether you intend to reside in the property. Evaluate the purchase price, location, and investment potential based on the area's demographics.

The location of your "-plex" property holds the key to its success. Embrace an area that resonates with your target tenant market and offers desirable amenities and opportunities for growth.

Intrigued by the surrounding population and demographics, you can unlock hidden secrets about your property's future prospects. Observe the pulse of the community, its crime rates, and economic vibrancy to make informed decisions.

As you set forth on this magical expedition, remember to embrace the spirit of N.A.V.I.G., for it shall illuminate your path to prosperity in multifamily real estate. May your endeavors be guided by wisdom and curiosity, and may your journey be filled with abundant rewards and enchanting discoveries.

In the forthcoming chapter, we shall unravel the enigmatic concept of the capitalization rate, an essential facet of real estate sorcery that will fortify your magical prowess. So, ready your wands of wisdom, and let us continue our journey into the realm of multifamily real estate.

CHAPTER 6: UNRAVELING THE MONEY MAGIC!

Okay, hold up! We're taking a little detour from the house hunt to dive into the mystical world of the capitalization rate! I know, it sounds like some fancy math thing, but trust me, it's a wizardry that every smart real estate investor needs to know.

The Magic Formula: Cap Rate Revealed

Get ready for some real estate sorcery! The capitalization rate (cap rate for short) is like a secret potion that helps you figure out if a property is making money or crying dollar tears. Here's the spell: Cap Rate = Net Operating Income / Market Value of the Property. Basically, it tells you how much moolah you're getting back for your investment.

Multifamily Magic: Why It's Special

Now, here's where the real enchantment happens. Multifamily properties have their own kind of magic when it comes to cap rates.

They're like the unicorns of real estate! Lower cap rates in a neighborhood mean it's a pretty safe bet, with property values going strong. Higher cap rates, on the other hand, could mean it's a bit riskier, but you might get bigger returns!

Enchanted Locations and Property Types

You guessed it—location matters! Big cities have lower cap rates because they're buzzing with people and all that city charm. Smaller towns, though, might have higher cap rates because they're still growing and changing. Also, new properties have their own special mojo, while older ones might need a little love and renovation.

Casting the Cap Rate Spell

So, now you know the cap rate magic, let's put it to work! You can use it to compare properties and see which ones sparkle with potential. It's like sorting through a treasure chest of opportunities!

When you're selling your place, knowing the cap rates of similar properties can help you figure out the best asking price.

Watch Out for Sorcerer's Traps

But hey, don't get too caught up in the magic. Cap rates have their limits, and they won't show you everything. They won't warn you about sudden economic craziness or unexpected repairs. And sometimes, folks might try to fudge the numbers a bit, so be careful!

Practice Your Money Magic

To become a real estate sorcerer, practice your cap rate calculations! You can start with triplexes that have cap rates above 7%—they're like magical training wheels! And when you're selling, use the cap rate mojo to find the right price for your property.

Remember, the cap rate is a neat trick, but it's not the whole story. Be smart, be cautious, and use all your real estate skills to make the best decisions.
With cap rate magic in your pocket, you're on your way to a land of real estate riches!
So, let's get back on our quest and find that dream property! Magical adventures await!

CHAPTER 7: THE QUEST FOR THE PERFECT PROPERTY

Alright, adventurers! We've had our fun with cap rates, and now it's time to get back on track—the search for your dream property! Finding that golden nugget might seem like a daunting task, but fear not! We've got the tools to guide you through this quest.

The Treasure Map: Finding Multifamily Properties

Now, where do you start your journey? Fear not, for there are many paths to the treasure! Online forums, real estate social groups, and good old-fashioned networking can lead you to valuable leads. But, in the realm of property hunting, you've got two options: embark on this adventure solo or seek a trusty companion to aid you.

The Lone Wolf Approach

If you choose to go solo, a world of benefits awaits! One major perk is cost—you'll save on commissions that usually go to brokers or agents.

That's more gold in your pocket! Your adventure will involve some legwork, like scouring real estate websites and local auctions. Keep an eye out for foreclosures too—they can be hidden gems!

Joining Forces with a Guide

No shame in asking for a guide, especially if you're new to the game! A seasoned realtor can be your trustworthy companion. They know the lay of the land and can help you find the best deals within your budget. They've got access to the Multiple Listing Service (MLS), a treasure trove of listed properties in the realm.

Searching for the Hidden Treasures

Whether you're exploring on-market or off-market properties, the landscape will change. On-market properties are listed by agents or brokers, and you'll find them on MLS websites like LoopNet, CREXi, and more. Off-market deals are where seasoned adventurers thrive. These rare gems are usually found through networking and contacting property owners directly.

Unusual Contacts and Mystic Resources

To uncover hidden gems, reach out to estate attorneys, builders, and wholesalers. They hold secrets to uncharted territories! Estate attorneys might know of owners willing to sell. Builders could reveal projects they've worked on or abandoned properties ripe for renovation. Wholesalers hold the keys to off-market deals.

The Magical 1% Rule

Ah, the legendary 1% rule! It's not a definitive spell, but it's a quick way to assess a property's potential. If the monthly rent is 1% or more of the purchase price, it might be a good investment. But remember, it's not the only charm in your toolkit. Cap rates and other calculations weave the full tapestry of your investment decision.

CHAPTER 8: THE HIDDEN TREASURES OF PROPERTY ANALYSIS

Hooray, fellow adventurers! You've stumbled upon a gem of a multifamily property that looks like a real steal! But before you whip out your gold coins and seal the deal, hold your horses for a moment. There's much more to consider before embarking on this investment quest.

Knowing the True Value

Setting off on a property investment journey without understanding its real value can be a grave mistake. You don't want to waste your hard-earned loot on a bad deal! So, before you swing that sword, always analyze and evaluate your potential properties. Take a closer look at the location, investment opportunities, profit potential, cash flow, and overall worth.

Revealing the Property's Potential

Determining a property's potential is a crucial skill during your initial assessment. You need to figure out how much treasure you can uncover from this investment.

Keep in mind that the property's location and appearance can greatly influence its value. Choosing a property in a shady area might not yield much return and could lead to unwanted troubles.

Assessing the Financial Landscape

Evaluating a property might seem like a daunting task, and it truly can be! Unless you're a skilled contractor or inspector, it's best to seek the guidance of experts. An inspector's report can give you valuable insights into the property's condition, arming you with strong negotiation tactics.

Evaluating Profit Potential

Once you've unlocked the property's investment potential, it's time to assess its profitability. Start by checking the purchase price and compare it with similar properties in the area. Factor in repair costs and closing expenses to get a clearer picture. Analyze the property's income, net operating income, and cash flow to see if it aligns with your investment goals.

Putting a Price Tag on the Treasure

To master the art of evaluating your multifamily property, apply the knowledge you've gained so far. Conduct thorough market research, evaluate repair expenses, and determine the expected net operating income. You can use the cap rate method to give the property a value, but remember, it's not a rigid rule.

The Mighty 50% Rule

Ah, the legendary 50% rule! It's a valuable tool for understanding operating expenses for rental properties. Simply multiply the property's rental income by 50%. Though not precise, it provides a good estimate of your potential cash flow. However, remember to conduct a thorough due diligence before making a final decision.

Armed with these skills and tools, you're now ready to unveil the true treasures of any multifamily property. Happy property hunting, intrepid adventurers! Your quest for lucrative investments has just begun!

CHAPTER 9: UNVEILING THE DEPTHS OF PROPERTY DUE DILIGENCE

When it comes to real estate ventures, mastering due diligence is paramount. This essential process involves a comprehensive examination of every facet of the property, ensuring that you make informed decisions and mitigate potential risks. In this chapter, we will delve into the art of due diligence, revealing the crucial elements to consider, and exploring the questions that can often be overlooked.

The Essence of Property Due Diligence

Property due diligence is the practice of delving deep into all aspects of the property you intend to purchase. It goes beyond merely scratching the surface and involves a thorough understanding of the property's physical condition, financial viability, and legal standing. As you progress through the buying process, there is typically a specified timeframe, usually 10 to 15 days, during which you can conduct your due diligence. However, it is advisable to start gathering information well before this period begins to be fully prepared.

Unraveling the Financial Aspects

During the due diligence phase, you must gain access to all pertinent financial information related to the property. Analyze the pro forma, which provides an initial glimpse into the property's financial performance, including gross rental income, repair costs, maintenance expenses, property taxes, insurance, and potential revenue losses due to vacancies or credit issues. Conduct a thorough market analysis to compare rental rates and property prices of similar properties in the area. Evaluate the demographic data to understand the target tenant population. Assess the property's potential for revenue growth and market stability.

Unearthing the Physical Reality

Conducting a comprehensive physical assessment is another crucial element of due diligence. Walkthrough each unit and inspect every aspect of the property to identify any existing issues or potential problem areas. Enlist the expertise of inspectors to thoroughly examine the property's utilities, potential pest infestations, and overall condition.

Put yourself in the shoes of a tenant and explore the surroundings, including common areas and parking spaces, to ensure tenant satisfaction and safety.

Navigating the Legal Landscape

The legal standing of the property requires meticulous attention during due diligence. Gather information on insurance claims, ongoing lawsuits, or any other legal matters that could impact the property. Review contracts with service providers, such as property management and landscaping companies. Verify that the property complies with all regulations and codes to avoid potential liabilities. Ensure that the title information is clear and free from any encumbrances.

A Comprehensive Due Diligence Checklist

To assist you in conducting a thorough due diligence process, consider the following checklist:

Physical Property:

> Conduct a detailed inspection of the entire property, including individual units.

> Explore the neighborhood during both day and night.

>> Request information on any needed repairs or outdated standards.

> Obtain Environmental Site Assessments and Reports, if applicable.

> Document nearby amenities and community assets.

> Note available services like laundry and internet.

>> Capture photographs and request recent property images.
>> Identify any energy-efficient features.

Financial Status:

> Request a comprehensive financial audit report.

> Conduct a detailed market analysis.

> Obtain a rent roll for all current tenants.

> Review present and historical property tax data.

Schedule a property appraisal.

Gather copies of all mortgages and lender information.

Obtain repair quotes from contractors.

Request documentation of operating income and expenses.

Create a real estate pro forma to project future financial performance.

Review records of any structural improvements made in the last five years.

Obtain salary and payment information for property service providers.

Request aged payables and receivable reports.

Legal Standing:

Obtain copies of leases and verify their accuracy.

Inquire about any pending litigation from the property owner and city.

Gather information on previous property-related lawsuits.

Obtain copies of all warranties.

Review compliance with the Americans with Disabilities Act.

Obtain property licenses, permits, and certificates.
Request a title report to ensure a clear title.

Equipped with this comprehensive checklist and the insights gained from this chapter, you are well-prepared to embark on the journey of property due diligence with confidence and diligence.

CHAPTER 10: MASTERING THE ART OF OFFER-MAKING

In this segment, we delve into the crucial process of making offers in the real estate realm. Chapters 8, 9, and 10 complement each other, forming a foundation for well-informed and strategic offer decisions. Let's explore the intricacies of making the right offer and the art of successful negotiation.

Preparation: Ready to Make Your Move

Congratulations on completing your due diligence and gathering valuable insights into the property's financial and physical aspects. Armed with essential information, it's time to make your offer. While sellers seek to maximize their profits, you must approach this step with a well-calculated strategy. Avoid simply accepting the seller's asking price without conducting a thorough analysis.

To begin, consider comparable properties in the area to gauge prevailing market rates. Factor in specific characteristics and income potential unique to your property. Utilize your capitalization rate and net operating income calculations to arrive at a reasonable sales price. Additionally, explore the property's replacement cost for an alternative perspective on its value.

The Art of Skillful Negotiation

Negotiation in real estate is both an art and a science. Every deal is unique, and understanding the seller's motivations can elevate your negotiation approach.

Are they eager to sell a foreclosed property quickly, or are they private owners looking to relocate? Knowing their intentions provides an edge during negotiations.

In competitive markets, swift action and offering slightly above asking price can set you apart from other investors. Presenting a well-thought-out plan to enhance the property's value or income justifies a higher offer. Conversely, in less competitive scenarios, lowballing can be effective if the property is overpriced or the owner seeks a quick sale.

Navigating Off-Market Opportunities

Discovering off-market properties, those not officially listed but available for sale, opens unique possibilities. Initiate conversations with sellers to gauge their interest and outline your offer through a letter of intent. Though non-binding, the letter serves as a starting point for negotiations. If both parties agree, a purchase and sale agreement can follow.

Making Your Offer on a Multifamily Property

Before making an offer on a multifamily property, gather essential components. Your letter of intent should detail the proposed price, earnest money deposit, financing terms, and findings from due diligence. Transparently communicate the time required for loan approval and closing. Share your investment experience and provide references if needed.

In Conclusion

Crafting successful offers involves research, calculated analysis, and adept negotiation skills.
With insights gained from due diligence, you can confidently navigate the complexities of real estate transactions.
Now is your moment to shine as you secure your ideal multifamily property.
Wishing you the best on this exciting journey of real estate investment!

CHAPTER 11: UNLOCKING OPPORTUNITIES IN MULTIFAMILY PROPERTY ACQUISITION

Now that you have thoroughly assessed the value and income potential of your desired multifamily property, it's time to dive into the exciting world of purchasing and financing. This chapter will guide you through essential considerations and options to ensure a successful acquisition.

Completing Due Diligence and Insurance

Before delving into financing, ensure your due diligence is comprehensive. Additionally, take the time to understand multifamily property insurance, as it differs significantly from primary residence insurance and can be costlier. Being aware of your coverage will help mitigate potential risks associated with property ownership.

Understanding Financing Terms

Familiarize yourself with key financing terms to navigate the process effectively. The interest rate represents the cost of borrowing money, expressed as a yearly percentage added to your monthly loan payment. Terms refer to the length of time for repaying the debt, with options ranging from short-term loans for property improvements to long-term loans spanning 30 years.

Exploring Financing Options

Multifamily properties offer various financing options.

Conventional mortgages from banks cater to properties with two to four units, while portfolio loans can consolidate financing for multiple properties. Government-backed multifamily loans, like FHA loans, provide additional support and flexible terms. Short-term financing, such as hard money loans, suits renovation projects.

The FHA Loan Process

For those considering FHA multifamily loans, understanding the process is crucial. FHA loans are designed to assist individuals who may not qualify for traditional financing. These loans focus on purchasing or refinancing properties, and down payments can be as low as 5%. Familiarize yourself with the requirements and benefits of FHA multifamily loans to make informed decisions.

Exploring Alternative Financing

In addition to traditional financing, there are other avenues worth exploring. VA loans can finance properties with up to four units for owner-occupied residences. State programs may also offer favorable terms for multifamily property buyers. Additionally, owner-financing can be a creative option, where the seller acts as the lender, simplifying the process and terms.

The Closing Process

As you approach closing, ensure all necessary preparations are in order. Review the contract with professionals and address any remaining details.

Choosing an experienced title company well-versed in multifamily properties is essential for a smooth closing. Properly handling security deposits is crucial to avoid complications during the process.

Embracing Opportunities in Multifamily Investing

Beyond traditional financing methods, innovative solutions and assistance programs are available to ambitious multifamily property investors. By exploring these options, you can unlock exciting opportunities and build a diverse and thriving investment portfolio.

With a clear understanding of financing and a strategic plan in place, you are ready to seize the opportunities in multifamily property acquisition. As you embark on this rewarding journey, remember to stay informed, remain adaptable, and make well-informed decisions for your long-term success in real estate investing. Best of luck on your multifamily investment endeavors!

CHAPTER 12: INNOVATIVE APPROACHES TO MULTIFAMILY PROPERTY INVESTMENT AND HOUSE HACKING

As you progress in your multifamily property investment journey, you may encounter situations where traditional financing options are not feasible due to limited capital for a cash offer or a substantial down payment. However, do not be disheartened, as there are creative strategies available to acquire properties with little to no money down.

Exploring Creative Investment Strategies

When traditional lenders are not an option, consider exploring private lenders, such as individuals like family, friends, or colleagues. They might be open to receiving a percentage of rent or partial interest during the loan repayment process. Additionally, you can leverage environmental benefits, like mineral rights or land parcels, to generate funds for a down payment.

Discovering the Power of House Hacking

House hacking is an excellent technique for multifamily property owners, allowing you to reside in one unit while renting out the others. This approach offers several advantages, including tax benefits, rental income generation, reduced housing costs, and wealth building opportunities.

Understanding Real Estate Crowdfunding

Real estate crowdfunding provides a platform to gather smaller investments from numerous investors, giving you access to more funds and networking opportunities. Demonstrating credibility with multiple investors can enhance your reputation with lenders and sellers. However, be prepared for challenges, such as building trust with investors and waiting for returns.

Types of Crowdfunding

Crowdfunding typically involves two types: equity investments and debt investments.

In equity investments, investors become shareholders and receive returns based on rental income or property sale proceeds. Debt investments involve investors lending money to property owners and receiving regular returns based on property income.

Noteworthy Real Estate Crowdfunding Platforms

Several crowdfunding platforms offer unique features and networking potential. Platforms like DiversyFund, Fundraise, and CrowdStreet have garnered attention in the industry. However, it is essential to thoroughly research each platform's offerings to find the best fit for your investment goals.

Strategic Partnerships and Real Estate Syndication

Partnering with other investors can be a valuable approach, as it allows you to leverage complementary skills and resources. Finding the right partner is crucial, as you will be sharing decision-making and financial responsibilities. Ensure that you establish clear boundaries, roles, and profit-sharing arrangements through a well-drafted partnership agreement.

Real estate syndication, a form of partnership, involves multiple investors pooling funds to purchase a property, with one person acting as the Sponsor. Syndication structures often utilize limited liability companies or limited partnerships.

House Hacking in Action: A Success Story

House hacking can yield remarkable results, as exemplified by Chad Carson's success story. By renovating a foreclosed fourplex, living in one unit, and renting out the others, Carson achieved positive cash flow and increased the property's value over time.

Embracing innovative investment options and house hacking can open up new opportunities for multifamily property acquisition. With a solid understanding of the DEALS formula (Decide, Examine, Acquire, Logistical Understanding, and Strategize), you can confidently pursue your investment goals and achieve long-term success in the multifamily real estate market.

CHAPTER 13: MAXIMIZING MULTIFAMILY PROPERTY PERFORMANCE

Once you become the proud owner of a multifamily property, the key to success lies in skillful management. Properly managing your property ensures high occupancy rates, well-maintained units, and increased property value, setting the stage for profitable future sales.

Essential Property Management Practices

For those new to the multifamily property business, taking things step by step is crucial. Start with a small property and learn the ropes carefully. Utilize multifamily management software to streamline rent collection, advertising, and tenant management processes.

Establishing Ground Rules and Complying with Legalities

Creating clear ground rules for tenant behavior is vital to maintaining a harmonious living environment. Ensuring compliance with local laws, eviction policies, and anti-discrimination regulations is essential to avoid legal pitfalls.

Determining the Right Rent Price

Setting the right rent involves careful consideration of factors like property updates, neighborhood demographics, and local rental market rates. The goal is to strike a fair balance that meets your investment objectives and tenant expectations.

Screening and Leasing Tenants

Thoroughly screen potential tenants by using technology for effective marketing and tenant identification. Employ screening questionnaires, credit checks, background checks, and interviews with previous landlords to find reliable tenants. A well-crafted lease agreement sets clear expectations and fosters transparent communication.

Nurturing Positive Tenant Relationships

Open and honest communication with tenants is the foundation of a successful landlord-tenant relationship. Timely response to maintenance issues, addressing tenant concerns, and providing necessary repairs contribute to tenant satisfaction and retention.

Maintenance and Property Enhancements

Regular property inspections are essential to identify maintenance needs and potential improvements. Stay on top of seasonal maintenance tasks and consider energy-efficient upgrades to attract environmentally-conscious tenants.

Financial Management

Financial management plays a critical role in successful property management. Calculate the operating expense ratio by dividing operating expenses by gross operating income. Aim for an expense ratio between 35% and 45% to indicate efficient operations.

Boosting Cash Flow

Increase cash flow by setting competitive rental rates based on amenities, location, and local market trends. Reduce operating expenses and explore additional revenue sources, such as vending machines and laundry services. Utilize strategic loan refinancing and debt management to optimize financial outcomes.

Effective property management is a blend of strategic planning, efficient communication, and proactive maintenance. By skillfully managing your multifamily property, you can build a robust and profitable investment portfolio.

LONG-TERM STRATEGIES

Now that you've become a multifamily investor, it's time to explore various investment strategies to maximize your property's potential. This chapter presents some fundamental approaches that can help you achieve your investment goals.

Investment Strategies:

Value-Add: The value-add strategy involves acquiring properties with potential for improvement. Investors focus on outdated or cosmetically challenged properties and make necessary upgrades to increase their value.

This approach may also include optimizing property management practices, adjusting lease structures, and strategically managing debt to enhance returns.

Opportunistic: Opportunistic investments carry higher risks but offer significant potential returns. Investors can pursue various opportunistic strategies, such as acquiring severely distressed properties and injecting substantial capital for improvements. Alternatively, investors may target properties in emerging areas with future development prospects, banking on increased property value over time.

Core/Core-Plus: Core investments are low-risk, stable properties in well-established markets with high-income potential. These properties are usually newer and require minimal improvements. Core-plus investments combine aspects of value-add and core strategies, involving properties with room for cosmetic or operational enhancements while maintaining a relatively low-risk profile.

The BRRRR Method:

The BRRRR method, short for Buy, Rehab, Rent, Refinance, Repeat, is a popular long-term investment strategy for multifamily properties.

Buy: Purchase a property with potential for improvement and positive cash flow. Consider properties in the B or C class range, which may offer upside and room for enhancements.

Rehab: Invest in property improvements and upgrades to add value. Enhance amenities, renovate rooms, and update essential features to attract quality tenants.

Rent: Once the property is rehabbed, focus on attracting good tenants through effective marketing and property management techniques.

Refinance: After the property's value has increased due to improvements, refinance the mortgage to access equity. This allows you to recoup the initial investment and allocate it toward the next property purchase.

Repeat: Repeat the process on another property, building a portfolio of cash-flowing properties and leveraging equity to expand your investments.

The BRRRR method is well-suited for multifamily properties due to the potential for multiple rental units to increase overall net income.

Investing wisely in multifamily properties requires careful evaluation, risk assessment, and effective execution of chosen strategies.
By incorporating these investment approaches, you can pave the way for long-term success and profitability in the multifamily real estate market.

�� **Special Offer!** ��

Loved Our Book? We're Excited To Give Back To Our Loyal Fans!

Get 5 Exclusive Digital Books For Free.

Email: infobookpub@Gmail.Com With The Subject As "Free Books"

www.ingramcontent.com/pod-product-compliance
Lightning Source LLC
Chambersburg PA
CBHW082231290526
45794CB00009B/3757